Kindness
Appreciation
Recognition
Encouragement

In the Workplace

By Lynn & Bru

D0968168

© 1996 by WE KARE

All rights reserved. No part of this publication may be reproduced in any form without written permission from WE KARE, P. O. Box 1613, Marshalltown, Iowa 50158

Library of Congress Catalog Card Number:
96-094268

ISBN 1-56383-058-2

Printed in the United States of America
G & R Publishing

Distributed By: CQ Products, 507 Industrial St., Waverly, IA 50677
319-352-2086

The KARE Book

We both feel that acts of kindness, appreciation, recognition and encouragement are important in all areas of our daily lives. Our work associates feel appreciated when another worker or the boss takes the extra time to recognize and encourage them. How often do we take the time to encourage and recognize others? We both feel this book is one way to help people in the workplace show kindness, appreciation, recognition and encouragement to each other. We have seen or been involved in many of these ideas. Additionally, we have included ideas provided to us by those individuals listed at the back of this book.

Lynn & Bruce Quernemoen
WE KARE

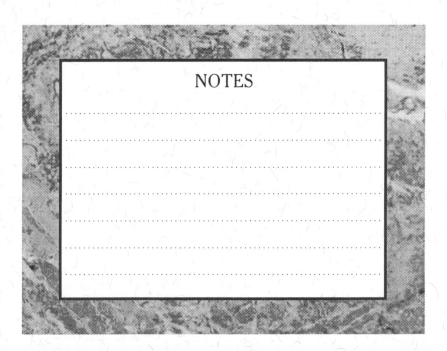

NOTES

FAX, E-mail, or send interesting articles concerning topics your customers may have an interest in.

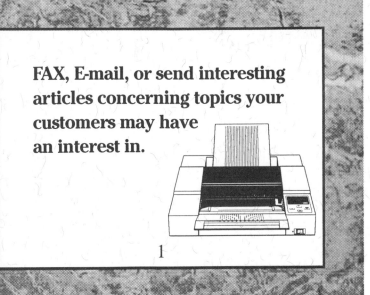

1

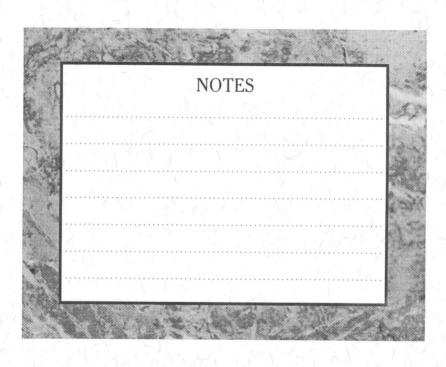

NOTES

Have a recognition event to recognize all employees who are involved in community service clubs, organizations or volunteer their time in the community.

"COMMUNITY SERVICE"

2

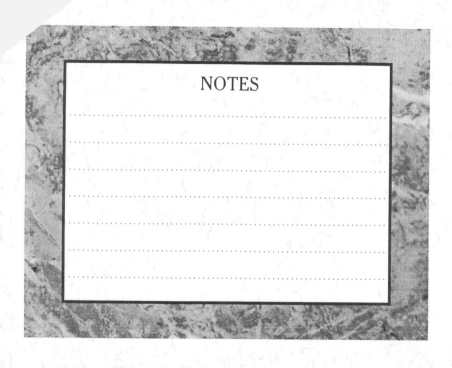

NOTES

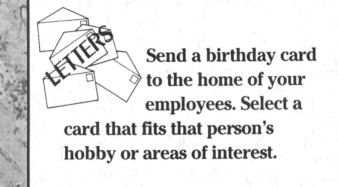

Send a birthday card to the home of your employees. Select a card that fits that person's hobby or areas of interest.

3

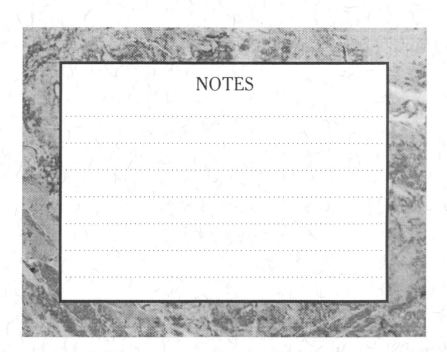

NOTES

Leave a handwritten note of thanks for those who clean your office or work area.

4

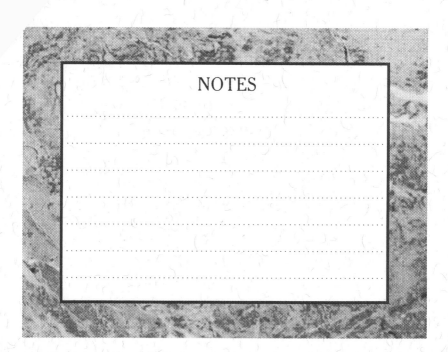

NOTES

Provide a recognition meal for your employees and their sons or daughters who are High School graduates.

5

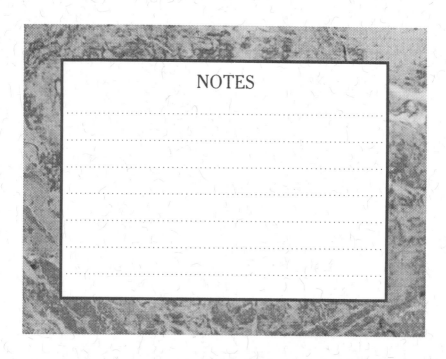

NOTES

Loan of your vacation home or cabin to fellow employee for a few days.

6

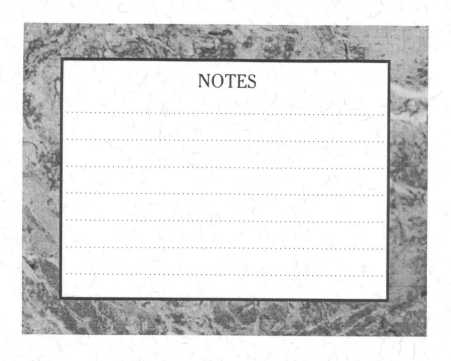

NOTES

. . . .

. . . .

. . . .

. . . .

. . . .

. . . .

. . . .

Get accomplishments of employees published in local newspaper or trade journals.

7

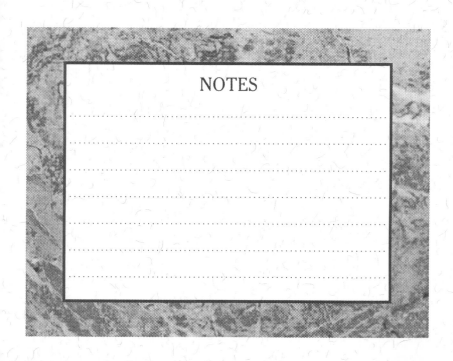

NOTES

Stop by your customer's office with donuts/bagels/juice, etc. for the staff with a small but visible display card indicating your personal thanks for their business.

8

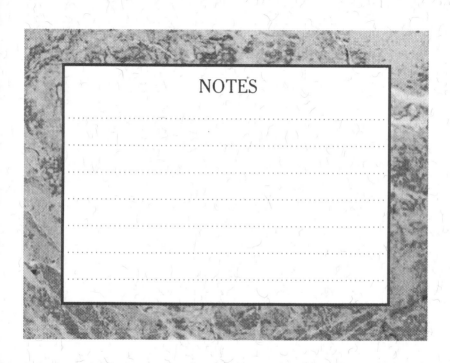

NOTES

. . . .

. . . .

. . . .

. . . .

. . . .

. . . .

. . . .

Notes of thanks to another group of co-workers attached to a helium balloon for each worker placed in the office or shop for a surprise one morning.

NOTES

Once a week, send a note of
thanks or appreciation to those
who have supported you or

who you have
noticed have
taken initiatives.

10

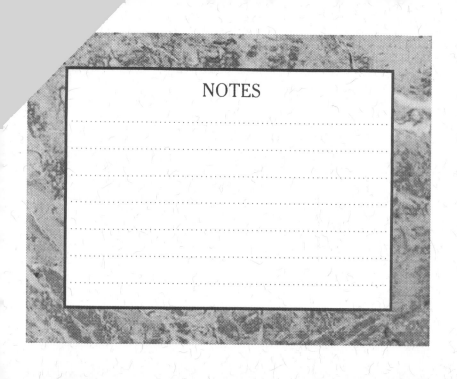

NOTES

 Once a month or every 2 weeks, post a picture of an employee listing information about them, such as birthplace, hobbies, children and ages, spouse and other jobs performed etc.

11

NOTES

**Plant Manager
invites employees
(invitation or sign up)
to a lunch for a time of com-
munication and employees
asking questions.**

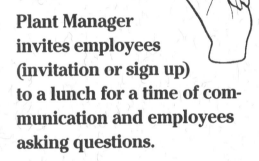

12

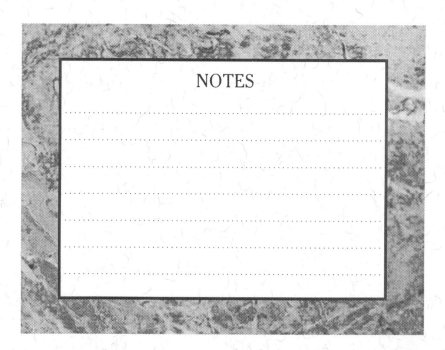

NOTES

ANNOUNCING

Host a supplier/vendor recognition event to give special awards; ie., Most Improved, Most Innovative or Proactive, have the highest ratings in areas of quality and on-time delivery etc.

13

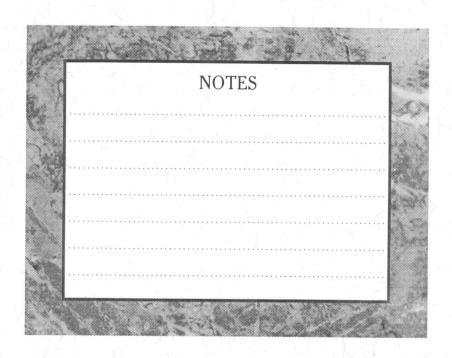

NOTES

Take the initiative and invite a new employee to lunch.

14

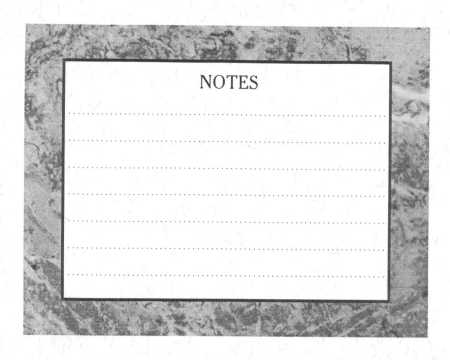

NOTES

TICKET

Give your NBA, NFL or college
sports tickets to an associate
and spouse for a game.

15

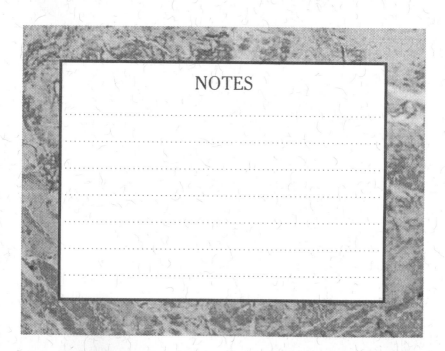

NOTES

Introduce your secretary as your assistant.

16

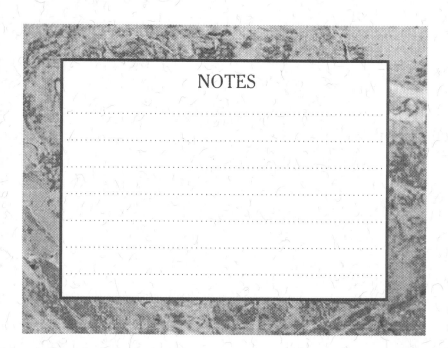

NOTES

GET WELL

Send a get well
card to employees who have
been off more than 2 days.

NOTES

Give a birthday gift to each customer.

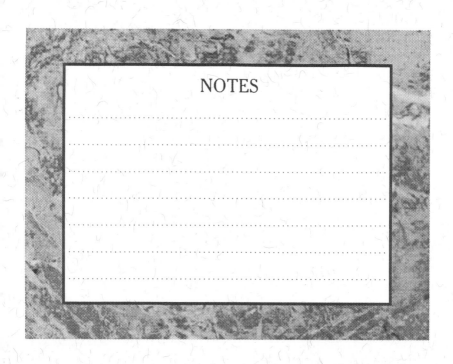

NOTES

Give out paperback books or audio tapes from motivational speakers or management theory.

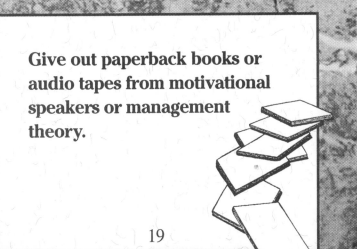

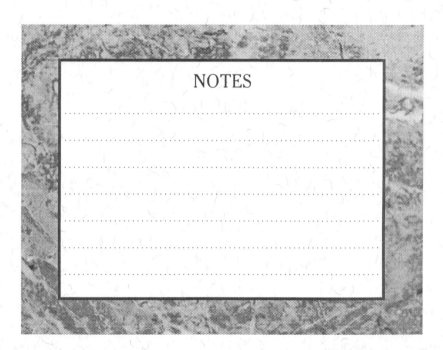

NOTES

When interviewing a potential new employee, get as many  people with him/her to receive their impressions. Then use this valuable input.

20

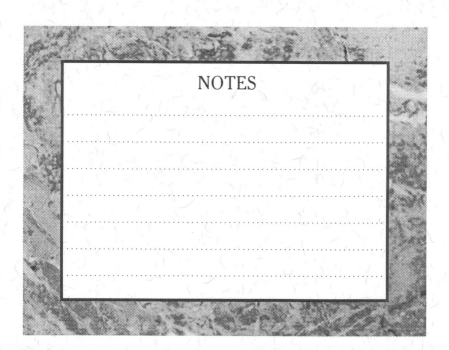

NOTES

....

....

....

....

....

....

....

After a hectic period of activity, shut down the office for a day and take everyone skiing, bowling or someplace fun and relaxing.

21

NOTES

CONGRATS!

Have the company President go to the employee's workplace to give out a 5 year anniversary award pin. Announce this over the intercom as it is occurring.

22

NOTES

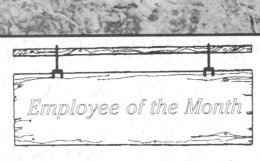

Employee of the Month

Provide a parking spot in front of the employee's building for the employee of the month.

23

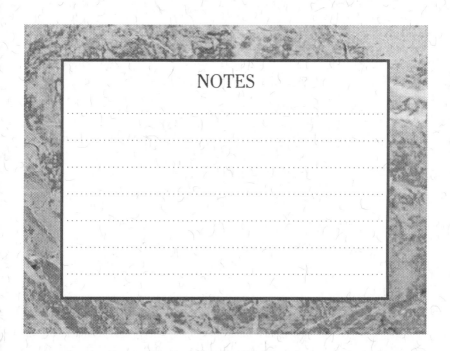

NOTES

....

....

....

....

....

....

....

Get your customers in for a
focus meeting and provide
lunch in some theme such as
Mardi Gras,
golfing,
fishing etc.

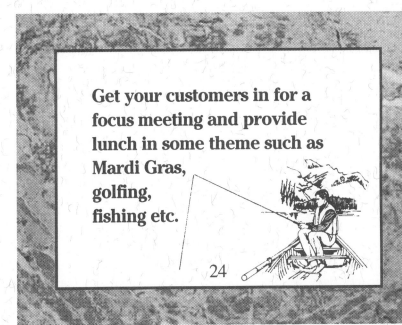

24

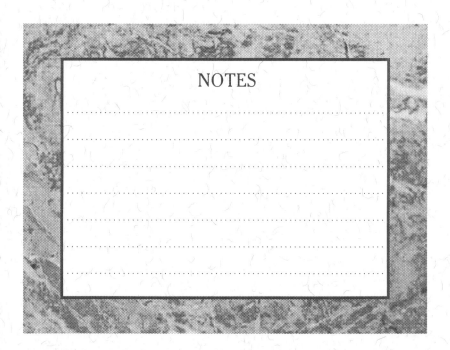

NOTES

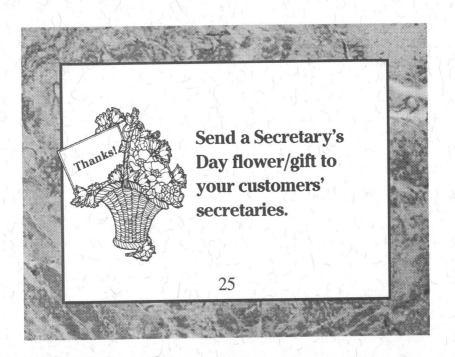

Send a Secretary's Day flower/gift to your customers' secretaries.

25

NOTES

When you come across an article in a magazine, newspaper or trade journal concerning a customer's company, cut it out and send it to your customer with a handwritten note.

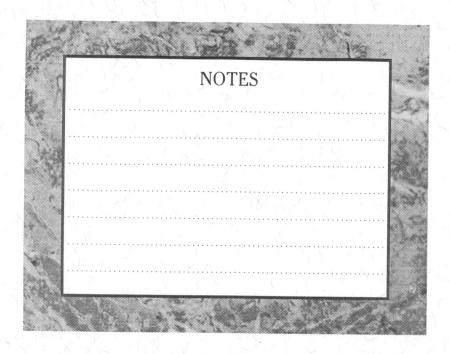

NOTES

Eliminate using words like employee, exempt, non-exempt. Rather, use words like co-worker, team member or associate.

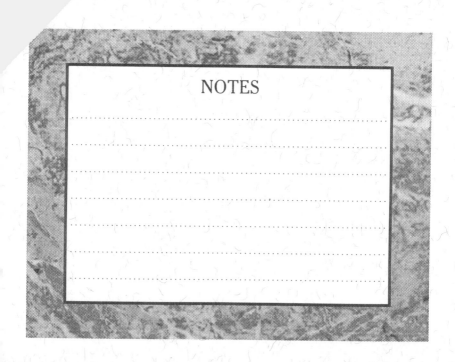

NOTES

Introduce someone that works for you as working "With Me".

NOTES

Set up a wall with an
individual picture of
each employee. List an
accomplishment of
each employee.

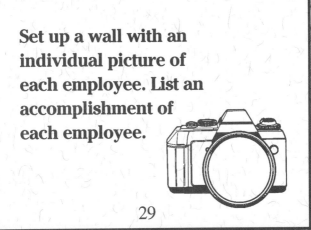

NOTES

Give a 60-second "Report of
Appreciation" at your regular
staff or department meetings
highlighting some recent
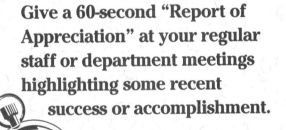
success or accomplishment.

30

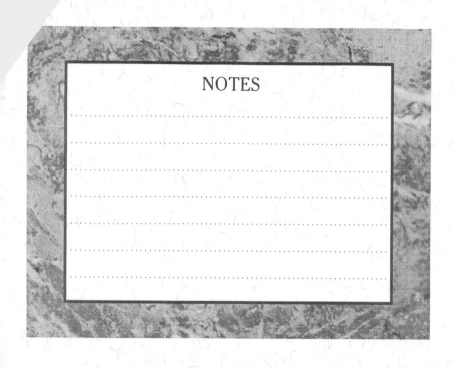

NOTES

Find out your customers' birthdays and send a Happy Birthday FAX to them.

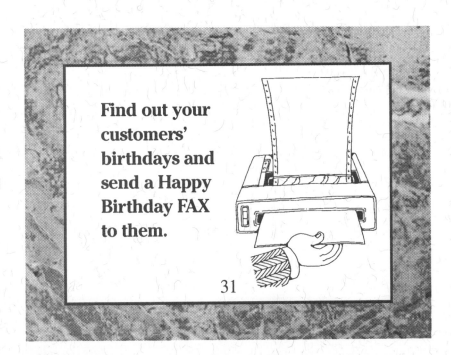

31

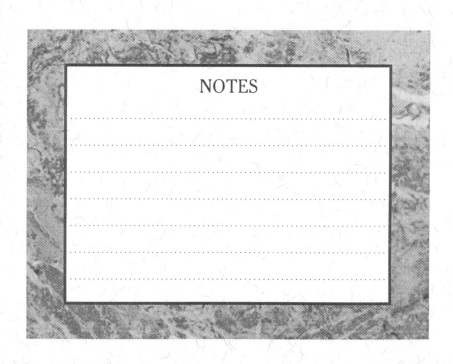

NOTES

. . . .

Stop by an employee's work area just to talk and find out how things are going; ie., children, family, outside activities.

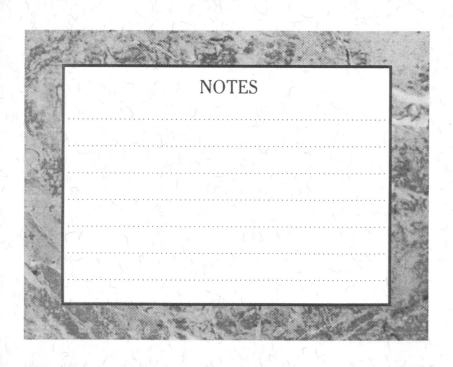

NOTES

. . . .

. . . .

. . . .

. . . .

. . . .

. . . .

. . . .

Tom,
Angie is a superior employee. I'm glad she's a part of our team!
-Al

Write a note of appreciation/ recognition to a manager in another department about one of the employees in his/ her department or team.

33

NOTES

Treat your staff to a special dinner or event after implementation of a major project.

34

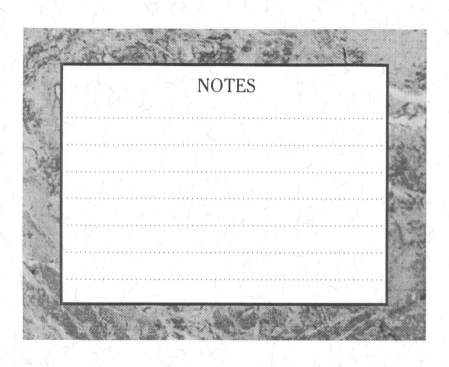

NOTES

Do something special for the wives of employees who travel and are gone a lot.

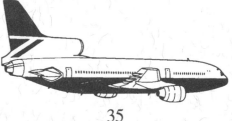

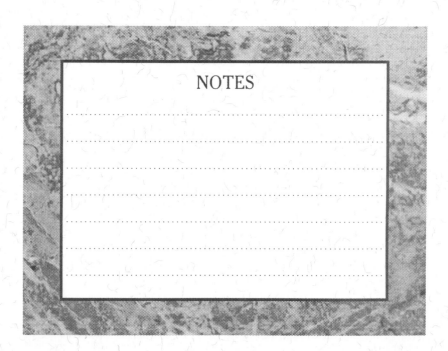

NOTES

Set up a recognition process to insure that, over a 12-month period, every employee has the opportunity to participate in group/team or individual recognition.

CALENDAR

36

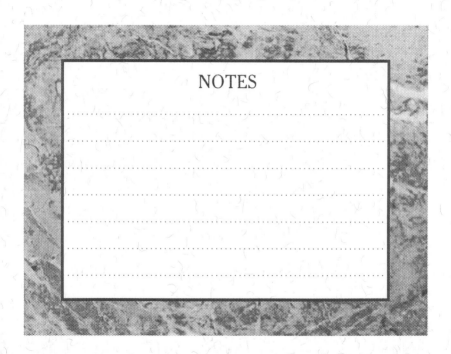

NOTES

Create a "Wall Of Fame" .
Designate a specific wall or
area where pictures of
employee recognition or "Atta-
Person" letters and certificates
can be displayed.

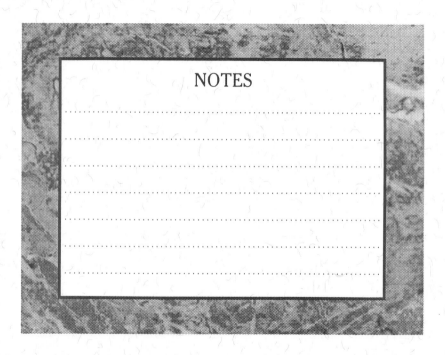

NOTES

Periodically have a dinner or lunch for all new employees to meet company management.

NOTES

. . . .

. . . .

. . . .

. . . .

. . . .

. . . .

. . . .

Take a survey of how
employees want to
be recognized. As an example,
one survey showed 87%
wanted a positive letter in the
personnel file whereas only
13% wanted an employee of
the month parking spot.

NOTES

Introduce an employee as a "Expert in _____".

40

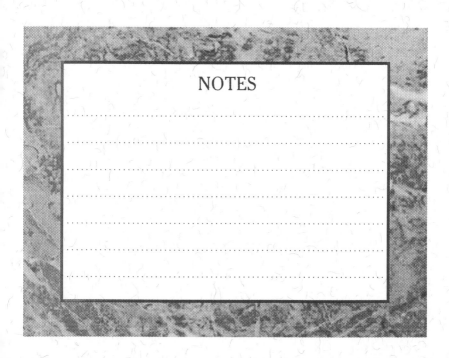

NOTES

Set up a "500 Club". Employee receives points for various aspects of work; ie., attendance, safety, cost savings ideas, community activities. When 500 points are attained, employee could receive an item like a shirt or jacket with the insignia "500 Club" on it.

41

NOTES

Print business cards for nonmanagerial employees.

JANE DOE
1522 ANYWHERE
ANYTOWN, USA

42

NOTES

Use these phrases and phrases like
these on a daily basis:
- That's a great idea.
- That was top-notch work.
- Thanks for completing the project.
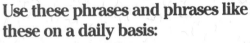
    - It's great working
    with you.
    - How can I help.

43

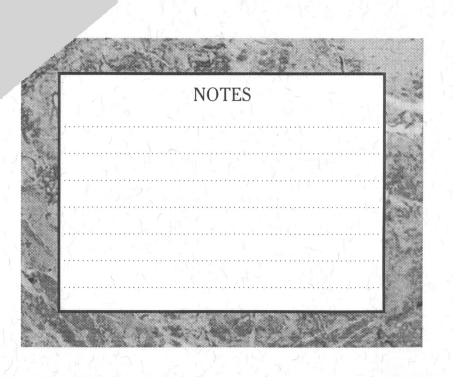

NOTES

Have an Employee Appreciation Day with Management greeting employees as they arrive and serve them all breakfast.

44

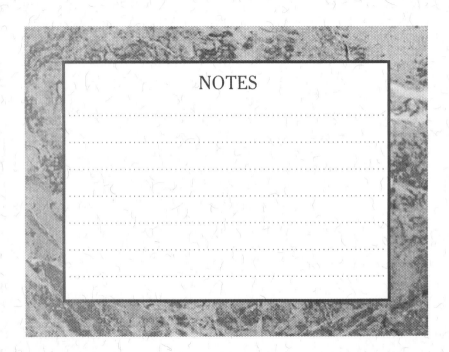

NOTES

. . . .

. . . .

. . . .

. . . .

. . . .

. . . .

. . . .

If you are wrong, admit it to
those at work who are impacted.

45

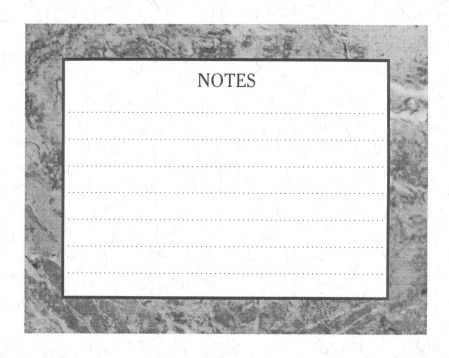

NOTES

Point out things to others that make your boss look good.

46

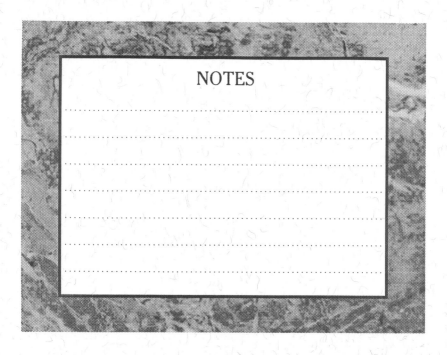

NOTES

Give words of thanks and appreciation in person for specific tasks well done.

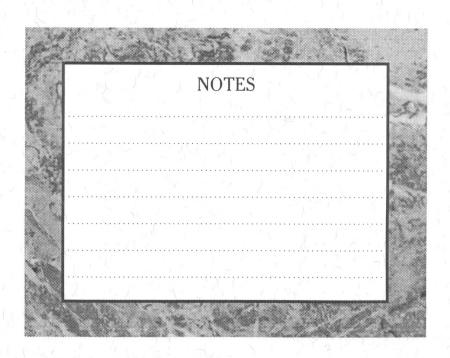

NOTES

Have a recognition banquet semi-annually or annually to recognize certain accomplishments.

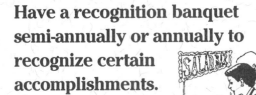

48

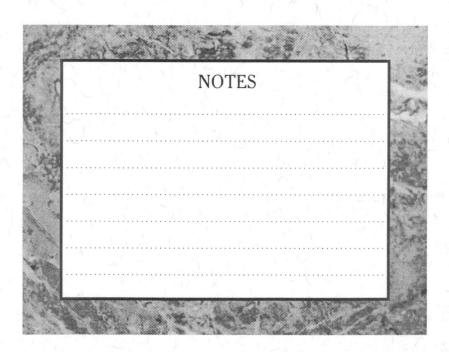

NOTES

**Bring in donuts or bagels for
the people you work with.**

NOTES

Set up a process that encourages employees to write short notes of appreciation to co-workers. Process could include easy-to-use form and maybe a small gift after an employee has received either 5 or 10 notes from co-workers.

50

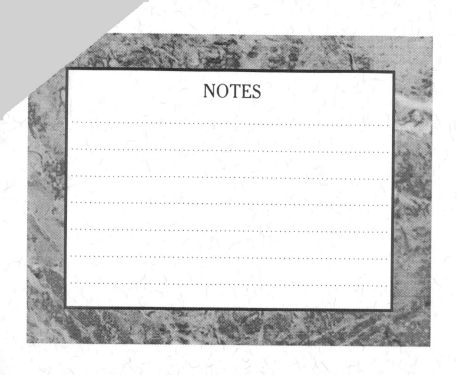

NOTES

Send flowers to office support staff (secretaries etc.) with a thank you note.

51

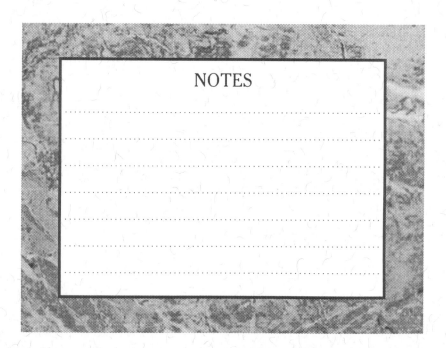

NOTES

Have an office Clean-up Day and have management picking up the trash and getting it to the dumpster. Make it fun.

52

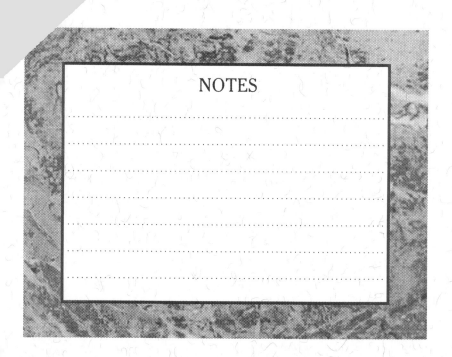

NOTES

Write a short note of
appreciation to someone in
your workplace who helped
support you in a recent project.

53

NOTES

GIFT CERTIFICATE

Give a restaurant gift certificate to individuals or teams that have met specific goals.

54

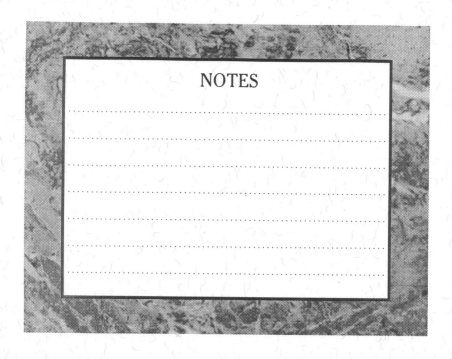

NOTES

....

....

....

....

....

....

....

This is your day!

Have a special Recognition Day for employees that have many years of service ie., 25 years, 30 years etc.

55

NOTES

. . . .

. . . .

. . . .

. . . .

. . . .

. . . .

. . . .

Give a birthday gift to each employee. Could possibly be a gift certificate to local store or Chamber of Commerce dollars.

NOTES

. . . .

. . . .

. . . .

. . . .

. . . .

. . . .

. . . .

Ask the people
you work with
over to your home for
a meal or social event.

57

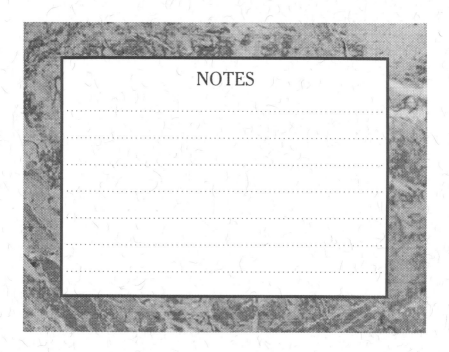

NOTES

**Take someone
you work with
out for a meal.**

58

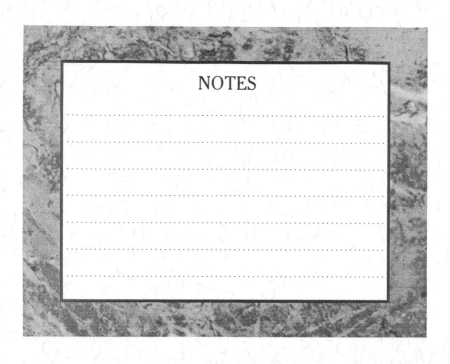

NOTES

Send flowers to the home of an employee or employee's spouse who had a new baby.

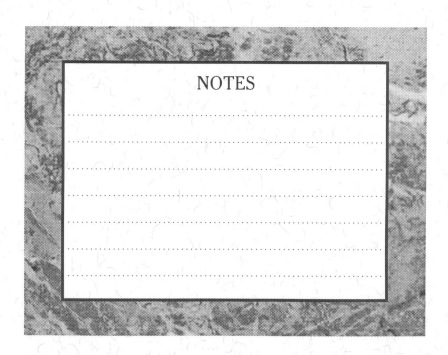

NOTES

Send a birthday card to your employee's college student or those in the armed forces.

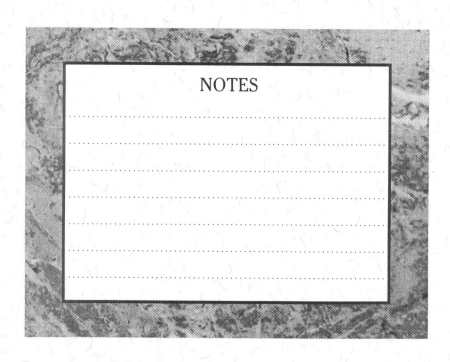

NOTES

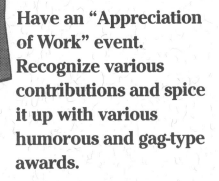

Have an "Appreciation of Work" event. Recognize various contributions and spice it up with various humorous and gag-type awards.

61

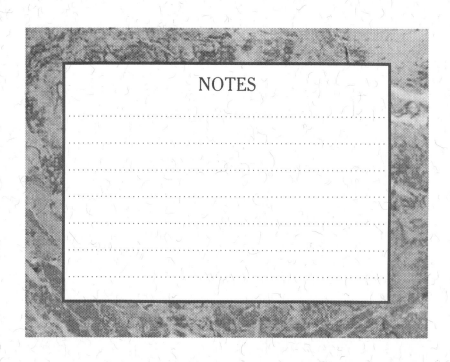

NOTES

....

....

....

....

....

....

....

news

**Recognition of employees
birthdays and length of service
anniversaries in newsletter.**

62

NOTES

Partner with a local school. Pair up an employee and student for a mentorship.

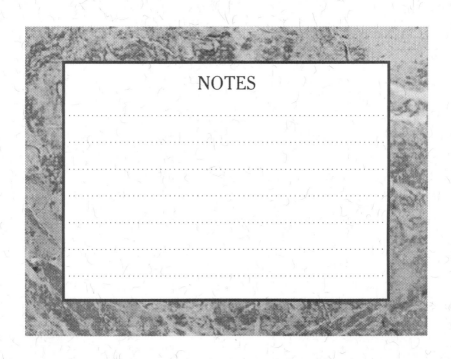

NOTES

**Bring in goodies
for break times
for employees
you work with.**

64

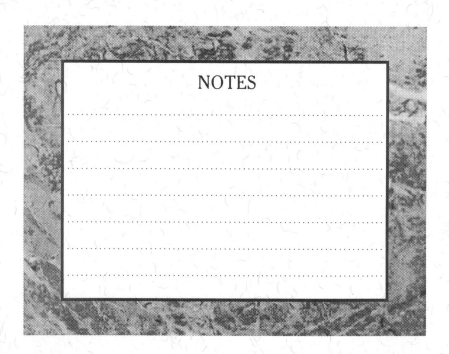

NOTES

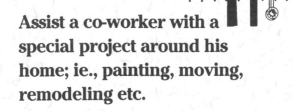

Assist a co-worker with a
special project around his
home; ie., painting, moving,
remodeling etc.

65

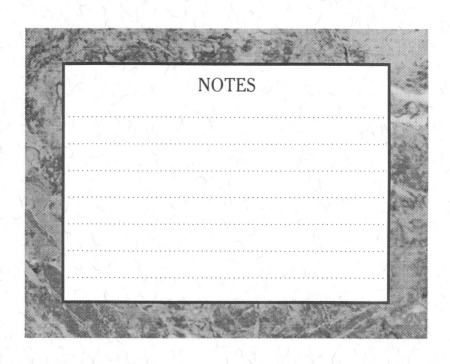

NOTES

Recognize those with perfect
or high attendance % or with
no-lost time accidents. This
could be for a month, quarter
or year.

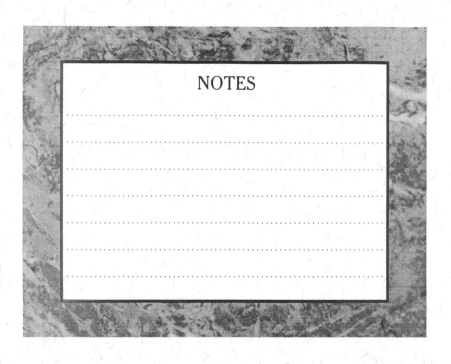

NOTES

Dinner out gift certificates for employees and spouses on special employment anniversaries.

67

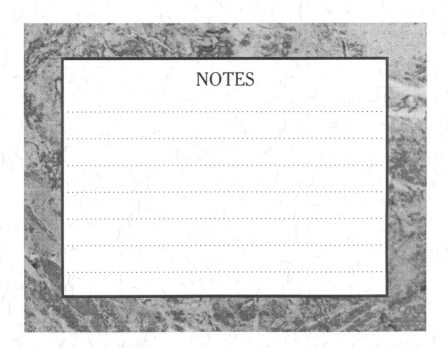

NOTES

Set up a wall in the office or
shop area with pictures of all
employees in their work-
groups, teams or departments.

68

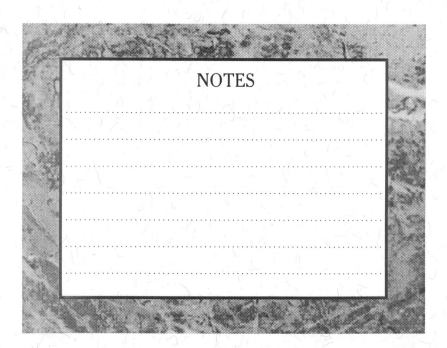

NOTES

Announce over the company intercom new orders received over a specific amount. Include customer, dollar amount and employee responsible for the order.

69

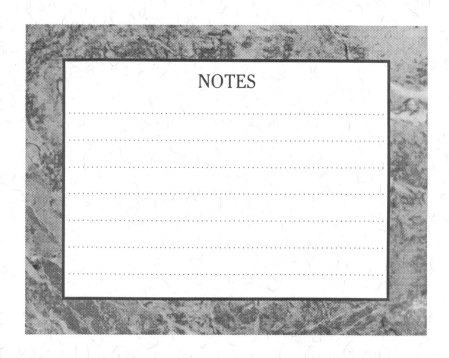

NOTES

Send a note of appreciation to the family of an employee indicating your appreciation for putting up with all the travel and time away from home.

70

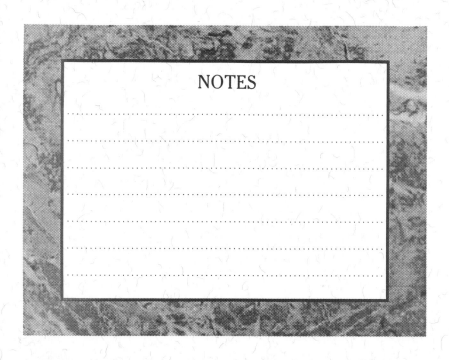

NOTES

Have ice cream
sundaes for all
employees for
achieving a very
recent plantwide or
department goal or
accomplishment.

71

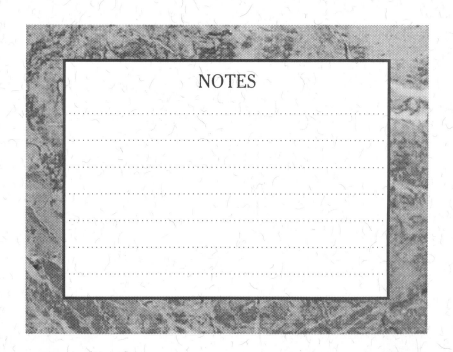

NOTES

. . . .

. . . .

. . . .

. . . .

. . . .

. . . .

. . . .

Use the company electronic mail to send a thank you to an employee for an accomplishment and copy other management personal.

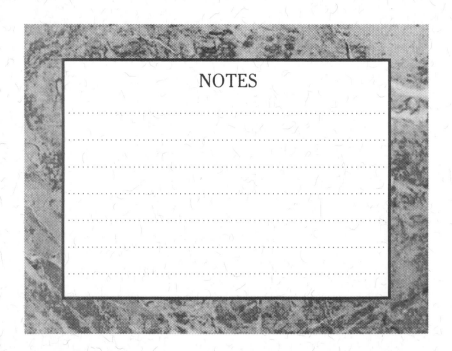

NOTES

 Have a costume dress up contest at Halloween and award prizes to the best dressed.

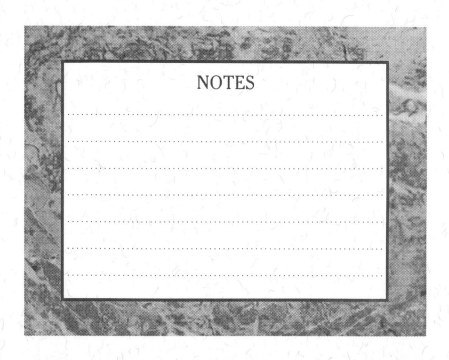

NOTES

....
....
....
....
....
....
....

**Do something special
for employees
birthdays; ie., day off,
1/2 day off, round of
golf or free lunch on
the company.**

74

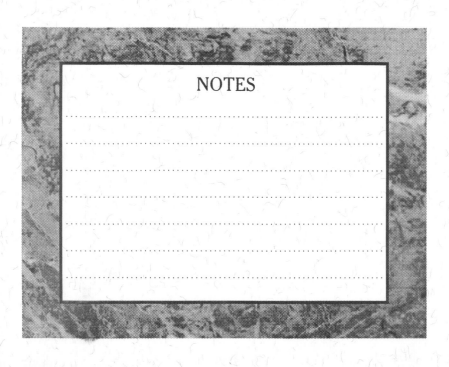

NOTES

To be effective, recognition programs should be set up to meet needs of various aspects of the workforce; ie. office, factory, outside sales, inside sales, young or old.

75

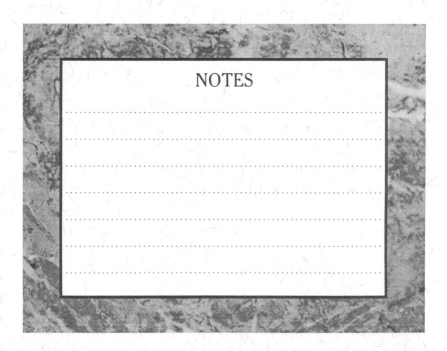

NOTES

Set up a Recognition Day for employees and families; ie., professional baseball game, amusement park, bowling or picnic.

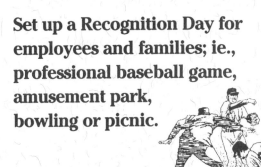

76

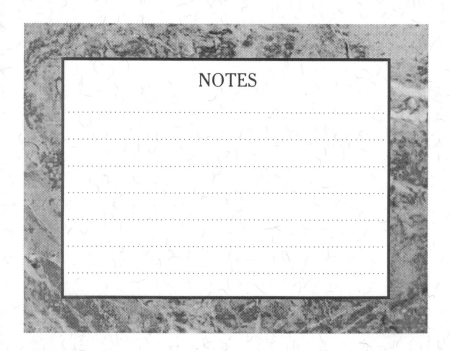

NOTES

. . . .

. . . .

. . . .

. . . .

. . . .

. . . .

. . . .

Let a salesman rent a luxury or sport car for a weekend or month in place of using the company 4-door sedan.

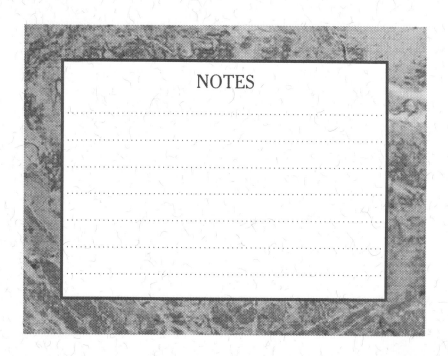

NOTES

Praise deserving employees at a department or all employee company meeting.

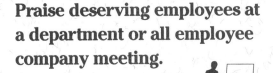

78

NOTES

Create a form or certificate with a heading "Pat On The Back", or "You Did A Great Job", etc. Make these available for all employees to use to send to a co-worker who has been a support.

NOTES

Each manager and supervisor is given a specific number of tokens each month which they give to employees on the spot for outstanding work. Tokens could be redeemed for gifts or meals at special local restaurants.

80

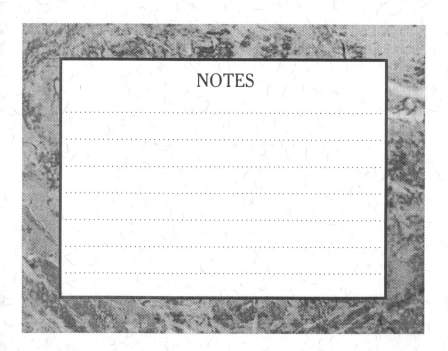

NOTES

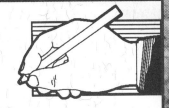

As a gift, give something that has been personalized, like a pen/pencil set with employee's name engraved on them.

81

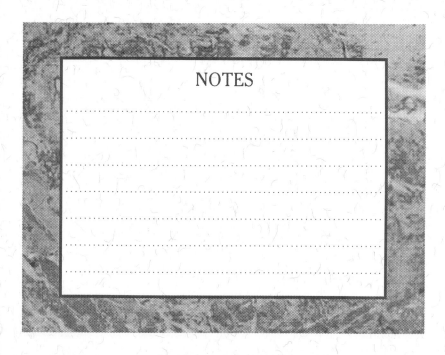

NOTES

**Send a card to your employees
on their wedding anniversary,
birthday or employment
anniversary.**

82

NOTES

....

....

....

....

....

....

....

To encourage
fitness, company
offers to pay part
of membership to
the local YMCA or
Fitness Center.

83

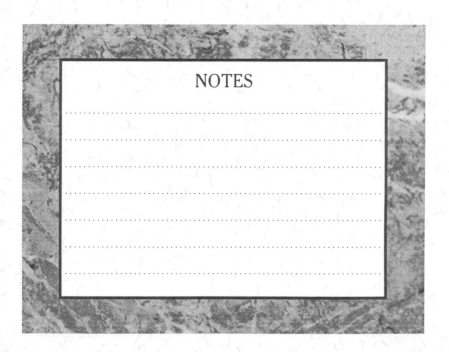

NOTES

Hand out "Certificates of Appreciation" spontaneously. These could be printed from a word processor or copied from a book of certificates.

Certificate of Appreciation

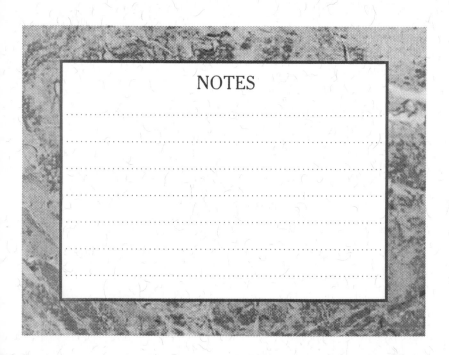

NOTES

· ·

· ·

· ·

· ·

· ·

· ·

· ·

Take out a full page newspaper
ad listing all employees who
are involved in community
service clubs or organizations.
If possible, include pictures of
employees.

85

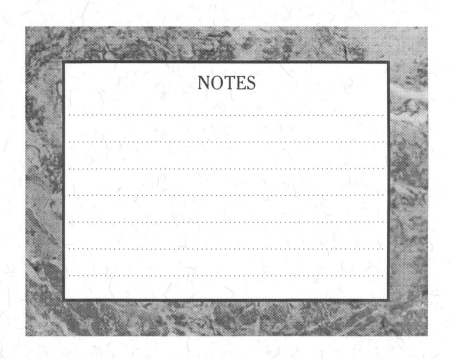

NOTES

Have a special dinner and
rooms for a weekend for
employees and spouses after a
successful project has
been completed.

NOTES

Do something special for an employees first anniversary ie., gift, day off, dinner out with spouse or lunch with someone in management.

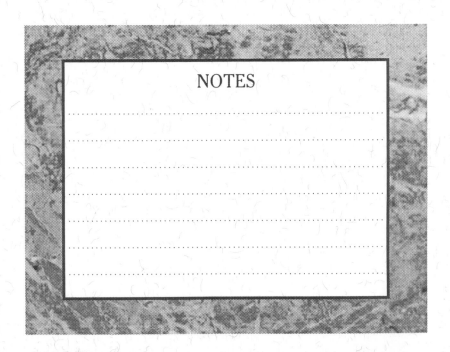

NOTES

Set up a supplier/vendor recognition process. Give out awards at the supplier/vendor location with all employees of the supplier/vendor present.

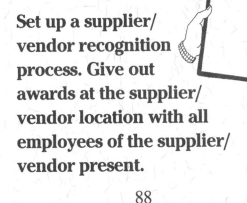

88

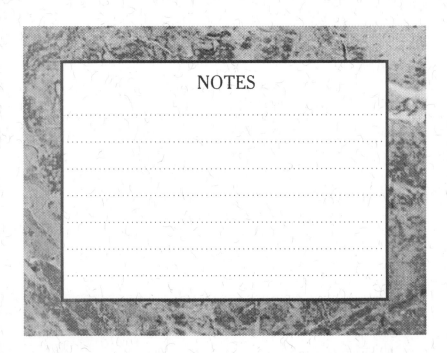

NOTES

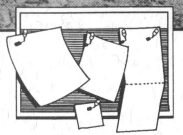

Set up an
employee bulletin board. Post
newspaper clippings and
pictures of employees who
have made the news.

89

NOTES

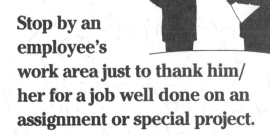

Stop by an employee's work area just to thank him/her for a job well done on an assignment or special project.

90

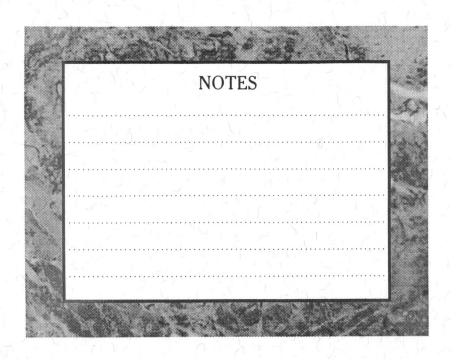

NOTES

....
....
....
....
....
....
....

Write a special note of appreciation and place in the employee's check or attach to the check.

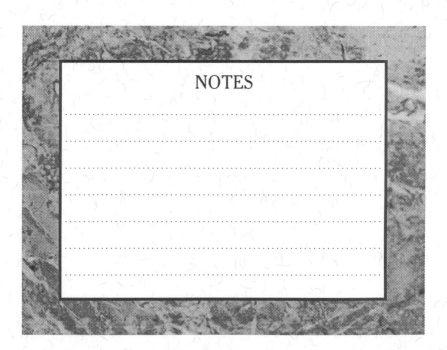

NOTES

Have a President, Vice President or Director call an employee to thank them for the good work on a special job or project.

92

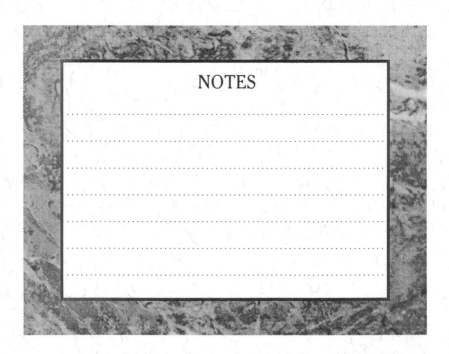

NOTES

Use caution when publicizing an individual's accomplishments. This may reward one employee and demoralize the rest of the group or staff.

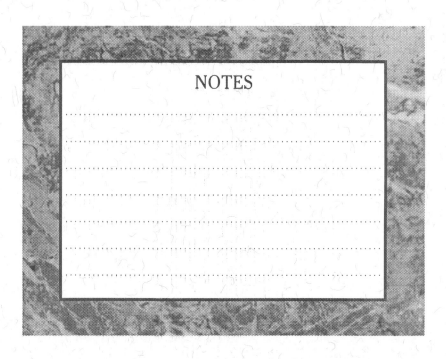

NOTES

Thanks to the following individuals that contributed their ideas to this book:

Carol Bator   Mary Burt
Carol Dorflinger   G. L. Grenert
Panda Kroll   Michael Machesney
Jeanne Anne Naujeck   Becky Neal
Brice Shanks   Rosemary Taylor

We are always looking and seeking out new ideas. If you have examples you would like to share, please write to us at:

WE KARE
P. O. Box 1613
Marshalltown, Iowa 50158-7613

Other Books on this topic are:

KARE in the Family

KARE in the Church